The Bane in Our Scars

By Ife Akanegbu

The Bane in Our Scars by Ife Akanegbu

Published by My Cute Prairies

Tumbler Ridge, BC

www.mycutestories.com

ISBN: 978-1-990633-14-0 (Paperback)

First Edition: July 2024

"We all have challenges; we all have things we struggle with. No one is immune, we are all predisposed. The battle isn't any easier on the other side. Where does it hurt the most? It hurts everywhere. The question "why me?" is asked by each and every one of us, only some ask this in the heart of darkness when the house is fast asleep. Each new day is a testament to the victories over yesterday's battle. Every man, pouched in a womb, is born into a battle and would only know absolute peace upon death. We didn't create these problems but we are designed thick enough to face them. Life is a gift; therefore, we should cherish it. But, why? Because today's victories are tomorrow's celebrations. Tarry awhile, don't go anywhere just yet."

Ife Akanegbu

The author wishes to acknowledge the insight and support of Charles Helm.

The dawn of a new day is the emblem of the victory achieved at sunset.

Table of Contents

Decisions should not be made in isolation at the convenience of the maker without a thought on the impact it would leave on family members, friends, associates, or anyone else who may be forced into a life they may never recover from. There are no la-la lands.

Preface

I attended medical school without fully grasping the significance of the mental health issues facing our society. I had learned the signs and symptoms and had a solid knowledge as to the treatment, but that was it. I had thought that mental health conditions were only for some people, not everyone, and that they were more common in other parts of the world than in our society.

During my psychiatry postings, I saw people with psychosis, but I could not recall the treatment administered. I had thought that the signs and symptoms had to be obvious, without realizing that mental health issues could be less apparent, similar to conditions like "hypertension." I also believed that mental illness only affected adults, not children, and that predisposed individuals were born with some physical deformity. I had no idea that anyone, including a well-dressed middle-class person, could be at risk.

However, I now understand that mental health is a crucial and wide-ranging topic without boundaries. I also know that early identification and treatment are essential. I have also realized that it is important to consider the consequences of our decisions on our loved ones rather than making choices in isolation. I have learned that making decisions in a positive state of mind leads to better outcomes, and giving up easily is not the solution.

Several governments enact policies to provide choices for those who feel they have reached their limit. While I respect this, medical assistance in dying should not be the first option for our suffering loved ones. We should explore underlying risk factors and provide as much help and support as possible. I believe we should walk with them, empathize, and provide reasons for them to continue their journey rather than accepting medical assistance in dying as the immediate solution.

Prologue

The bitter tang of the antacid coated Frederick's tongue, but the burning in his stomach refused to subside. He popped two more tablets, their chalky taste filling his mouth. A wave of nausea washed over him, forcing him to double over momentarily.

As he waited for the after-effect, a muffled giggle drifted upstairs, followed by Martha's footsteps. He fumbled to shove the empty packet into his pocket, hoping it wouldn't be the first sign of something amiss.

The doorknob rattled. "Honey?" Martha's voice chimed, laced with a hint of surprise. "Everyone's here already! The party is about to start just as we had planned."

Frederick forced a smile, the action sending a jolt of pain through his abdomen. "Coming down in a sec," he called, his voice strained. He waited until her retreating footsteps faded before venturing towards the bedside dressing table.

Glancing in the mirror, he saw what Martha might see – the pallor in his usually tanned face, the dark circles under his eyes. He straightened his rumpled t-shirt, a futile attempt to erase the growing unease within.

Downstairs, the festive hum of party chatter reached him. Guests had begun arriving for his 50th birthday bash, thrown by his ever-enthusiastic wife Martha. He winced as he tried to smile, the effort sending a spike of discomfort through his abdomen.

The evening unfolded in a muted haze. Laughter and conversation felt like distant echoes, punctuated by the dull ache gnawing at his insides. He kept brushing it off as indigestion, a side effect of too much barbeque perhaps. Yet, the clinking of his fork against the plate seemed amplified, the weight of the birthday cake overwhelming as he attempted to cut it. The knife slipped from his grasp, clattering to the floor with a jarring finality. Nervous laughter bubbled around him, masking a flicker of concern in Martha's eyes.

As the music swelled, inviting them onto the dance floor, Frederick forced a smile. He held Martha close, her familiar warmth a comforting anchor in the sea of unease. But halfway through the slow dance, the pain intensified, a searing fire ripping through his stomach. He gasped, his smile contorting into a grimace.

"Martha," he rasped, his voice barely a whisper. "Something's wrong."

Concern bloomed in her eyes, replacing the amusement of moments ago. "What is it, honey?" she asked, her voice laced with worry.

He wanted to lie, to brush it off as nothing. But the pain was a rising tide, threatening to drown him. "I don't…" he started, then stopped. The world tilted, the music morphing into a cacophony. He lost his balance, crashing to the floor with a grunt.

Martha gasped, dropping to her knees beside him. "Frederick!" she cried, panic replacing concern. "What's happening?"

Through the haze of pain, a single, primal thought roared through his mind. "Kyle," he groaned, clutching his stomach. "Call Kyle…please…I don't want to die!"

The party lights blurred into a kaleidoscope of colours, the festive music replaced by his ragged gasps for breath. In Martha's tear-streaked eyes, Frederick saw not just confusion and fear, but a flicker of understanding – the recognition of something monstrous lurking where there should have been only good health and years more to come.

Cracks in the Armour

Kyle's smile was a stiff but well-worn mask, practiced over a decade of delivering difficult news. The tightness in his chest battled for dominance as he prepared to enter the consulting room. He stood just outside the door, letting out bated breaths at the same rhythm of his heartbeat. He had been an oncologist for up to a decade now and had worked with so many cancer warriors throughout the years but something about this one seems a little too close to home.

The nurse walked past him giving him a "Should I?" look as he nodded his consent. Then she walked in first and he knew it was only a matter of time before his attention was needed.

"The Doctor would see you now." He heard her say, lifting his smartphone towards his face to make sure his enthusiastic mask was glued on tight. Then with one last fill of his lungs, Kyle tightened his grip on the door handle, its cold metal biting into his skin as he stepped into the precipice of the unknown.

"Whoa, that was such a hectic procedure," was the first thing Kyle said to his patient. "I hope it wasn't too overwhelming for you."

"Trust me at this point, anything is better than Cytoxan," the two men let out a cautious laugh as they both went in for a hug.

"So Frederick, how have you been?" Kyle found his seat, noticing his friend arrived alone, a flicker of worry creasing his smooth façade. "Wait, where's Martha?" he asked, a touch too casual.

Frederick shifted his gaze to the chipped floor tiles, tracing the spiderweb cracks with his worn shoe. "She's...busy nowadays I guess." The words hung between them, heavy and accusatory. All through Kyle's career, he never expected this kind of phrase from any of his patients when they addressed their wives. What's more, these people weren't just patients, they were longtime friends and he felt the obligation to fix their problems.

But instead, Kyle waited, the silence, a heartbeat too long, and the air thick with unspoken dread. Frederick noticing this decided to look up, as if the vibrancy had been leached from his eyes, replaced by the desolate landscape of a man waging a war he feared was already lost.

"Tell me straight, Doc," his voice was a cracked whisper. "The last tests...they weren't good, were they?"

Kyle hesitated the hope of the PET scan they had just done heavily in his mind. He'd already seen the shadows in the previous images, the hints of disease spreading relentlessly. "Well there isn't a lot I can tell you now but we need to wait and trust that today's scan would come out the way we hope. It is only then we can conclude on your prognosis and offer lasting solu—"

"No," Frederick cut in, a sharpness spewing in his resignation. "Just tell me. Is it worse? Am I dying?"

The question echoed against the bare walls, each syllable a death knell. Kyle's well-rehearsed words of practiced optimism faltered. "Cancer...it's aggressive. Stage three as we had noticed the last time. This scan is important to give us a clearer picture of what we are fighting against, to plan the next steps, but…"

The rest of his sentence drifted away, lost in the void of Frederick's devastated expression. The fight drained from his patient, revealing a raw vulnerability Kyle rarely witnessed.

Frederick's voice trembled, barely audible over the rhythmic squeak of a nurse's rubber soles in the hallway. "My marriage...was far from being perfect before this, but pancreatic cancer only made our lives worse. It's like… the other day, I was so exhausted after chemo, just wanted to close my eyes. Then Martha started arguing about some chore I hadn't finished. A small thing, but... from the tone of her voice I knew…" He swallowed, his eyes glistening. "It wasn't the chore, Doc. She looked at me with... not disappointment, but disgust. Like I was just lazy, not sick." His voice caught on a choked sob. "And now...what if I'm getting worse? Would we ever make it then…" His voice trailed off, the unspoken fear more terrifying than any medical diagnosis.

Kyle, an oncologist, and veteran of countless such battles, felt his armor crack. No clinical textbook he'd ever read or medical trial, held the answers to mend a crumbling life...or a broken heart.

Echoes of the Unforgiven

Kyle collapsed onto the couch, the weight of the day settling into his bones like sandbags. An ache throbbed in his shoulders like a constant metronome marking the relentless hours spent hunched over bodies, battling disease with a precision that left little room for his fatigue. He closed his eyes, the darkness a momentary oasis before the world inevitably rushed back in.

His fingers grazed his phone at the sound of the incoming notification, the gorilla glass cool against his clammy skin, a brief respite from the relentless warmth of the hospital. He scrolled listlessly, eyes scanning the mundane updates of daily life, punctuated by a jarring news alert about staffing shortages and overnight emergencies. Kyle swiped it away, the familiar knot of work tightening in his chest.

Seeking a distraction, his thumb hovered over the familiar green app, a lifeline to a time before his world narrowed to sterile hallways and relentless clocks ticking beside patients' beds. His college alumni chat group, a usually jovial stream of memories and career updates, now pulsed with a bright yellow banner.

"Toronto University presents… Med school Annual Reunion Party!" it screamed in a sickeningly cheerful font. The date slammed into him, a visceral blow that echoed through his exhausted mind. It was the day Martens died.

Grief washed over Kyle like it had done all those years ago, tinged with a guilt that still burned raw beneath the surface. It took him some time to notice but just underneath the title was something else written in tiny fonts "In loving Memory of our beloved Classmate and Friend, Martens Tennant Jnr." Images, sharper than any anatomy textbook illustration, flickered in his mind: the frantic ring of his phone that jolted him awake from his drunken state, a dash to the ER, the icy dread that had consumed him during that endless night. And then, the chilling dawn, the weight of someone's life slipping through his fingers.

The faces of his classmates grinned out at him from the reunion poster, their cheerful smiles a stark contrast to the emptiness that lingered in Martens' place. A pang of longing pierced through his weariness. Perhaps, just for a few hours, he could recapture the ease of those years, the certainty of their shared dreams of being doctors before the cold realities of medicine had chipped away at their youthful idealism.

But another, more insistent voice whispered warnings, a voice forged in countless sleepless nights and heart-wrenching conversations. He'd tried attending his best friend's funeral shortly after the death but It had left him feeling hollow, his grief swallowed by a performative display of sadness from their other colleagues. People who couldn't give Martens the light of day while he was alive, kept bawling out their eyes talking about the "Dangers of Depression" while taking some "Memories" to post on their socials.

No, he wasn't ready to revisit that.

"Honey, dinner's almost ready." Julie's voice, normally a grounding presence, startled him from his turbulent thoughts. She had also been staring at his phone screen as he lifted his head, meeting her gaze. The worry etched into her features mirrored his inner turmoil. She had known the exact date, knew the shadow it cast in their lives. With this knowledge in mind, he felt like this was an opportunity to reach out, to share the burden of memory, but the words felt lodged in his throat, heavy and unspoken.

Julie set the plate down, the scent of his favorite pudding a comforting aroma in the quiet of their kitchen. A gentle hope flickered in her eyes as she decided to intervene. "Wow, a reunion, how nice... I can't remember when we had one of those... " There was a tentative curiosity in her voice, an unspoken plea for him to break the invisible barrier he'd erected around this anniversary. Then she added, "Are you thinking of going?"

Kyle stared down at his plate, his fork tracing meaningless patterns in the untouched food. The thought of the reunion – the forced smiles, the small talk, the inevitable rehashing of the past – constricted his throat. "I don't know," he mumbled, his voice thick with the weight of unspoken anxieties.

Julie reached out, her hand covering his, the warmth a stark contrast to the cold that seemed to have settled within him. "It might be good for you, Kyle," she said softly. Her intuition was a sharp blade, cutting through his defenses. He knew she sensed there was something more than his usual aversion to socializing fueling his reluctance this time.

The silence stretched between them, broken only by the soft ticking of the kitchen clock. It pulsed in his ears, a relentless countdown to an explosion he could feel brewing in his chest.

Her words, well-intentioned but ill-timed, ignited the fuse. "It's just a reunion, Julie." The words came out harsher than intended, tinged with the bitterness of exhaustion and the sting of too many difficult memories.

Julie's eyes widened, a flicker of hurt crossing her face. "...And a memorial for your dead roommate. I thought you guys were close, Kyle," she said, the familiar note of disappointment in her voice a barb he couldn't deflect.

Kyle surged to his feet, the chair scraping against the floor a jarring discord against the taut silence. "Close?" His voice was a jagged edge, the word echoing his internal conflict. "Well pretty much but It's not that simple, Julie! You don't get it!"

His hands flew up in a futile gesture against the crushing weight of hers and unresolved guilt. The years he'd spent shielding himself from the full, messy truth of Martens's death came crashing down, leaving him exposed and vulnerable, a gaping wound laid bare under the harsh fluorescent kitchen lights.

They were words hurled in the heat of the moment, words born of desperation and the lingering ache of loss. Yet, even as they hung in the air between them, he felt a twist of shame. Julie, her shoulders slumped in sudden defeat, mirrored his exhaustion. Silence descended, the unspoken pain echoing louder than any argument. It was a gulf he could not bridge that night.

A Sprint to the Finish

The air was crisp, each breath a tiny cloud in the pre-dawn chill. Usually, Frederick relished this hour, the quiet streets echoing with his footsteps. But this morning, something was off. His body felt heavier than usual, every stride demanding an effort he was no longer accustomed to.

Kyle was beside him, a steady presence. Despite their difference in build, they had always kept a comfortable rhythm. Today, however, Frederick fought to match his friend's pace, the silence between them a chasm he couldn't seem to bridge.

"Remember when we ran that 10k?" Kyle broke the tense quiet, his voice too cheerful. "Thought we'd never make it past the halfway mark." An image flashed through Frederick's mind of the celebratory beer afterward, and a sharp pang of longing sliced through him for a body that felt invincible mere months ago.

He forced a laugh, the sound brittle in his ears. "We were unstoppable then, weren't we?" The words, while true, held an underlying hollowness. The old energy was missing, replaced by a weariness that mirrored the graying sky overhead.

"Yeah, and I bet we can still do it now." There was an awkward silence settling between them. "It's not that hard. Slow and steady wins the race, right?" Kyle grinned, his face flushed – a stark contrast to Frederick's pallor. A flicker of guilt pricked at Frederick's conscience. Kyle meant to be encouraging, but it only emphasized the relentless change that had taken hold of him.

Desperate for a distraction, Frederick fumbled for his worn iPod. "Let's bring a little life back into this run, yeah?" With practiced ease, he shuffled through his favorite playlist, landing on a familiar beat. "Nothing some great music can't fix." He said as Katy Perry's voice belting "The one that got away!" filled the space between them.

A smile tugged at Kyle's lips. "Alright Perry, this is not a bad song!"

Frederick shared his earbud with Kyle, a silent bond between them. For a fleeting moment, the world receded, filled with the upbeat pulse and lyrics that spoke of uninhibited joy. They'd always shared a fondness for pop music, a guilty pleasure against their serious medical personas.

"You know during Martha and my wedding reception," A wistful note crept into Frederick's voice. "We played this song on repeat. It happened to be both our favourites so we couldn't get off the dancefloor the entire night. I always swore I had two left feet, but that night…" He paused, the memory vivid in his mind's eye – Martha's laughter, the vibrant blur of their friends, the feeling that he could conquer anything. Then he punctuated with a sigh "Those were some really good old days."

Sensing the undercurrent of sadness, Kyle bumped his shoulder. "You know what? Maybe we could catch a live concert one of these days, yeah? Blow off some steam. You, me, Martha... I hear Katy is coming to Canada soon." Kyle's voice held a note of forced optimism as if he could bring Frederick's old energy back into existence. The suggestion, well-intended, hung awkwardly between them.

The old Frederick would have jumped at the idea. But now, an image flashed in his mind – a crowded stadium, the pulsating lights, the jostling bodies. Weakness washed over him, an invisible weight far worse than any chemotherapy drip. He stared down the long stretch of trail, the image of a chaotic concert flashing through his mind. The energy required for such extravagance now seemed impossible. "I... I don't know," he mumbled feebly, searching for an excuse that wouldn't reveal his true terror.

Kyle slowed his pace, a crease appearing between his brows. "Come on, Freddie, it would be fun! Shake things up a little."

Each word landed upon Frederick like a pebble, piling on a steadily increasing weight. "Fun" was a concept that seemed to belong to a different life. Besides, what if he made a fool of himself, unable to stand for even a song? The humiliation felt unbearable. "Really, Kyle?" he hedged. "You're my doctor, you of all people should know that fun is the least of my priorities right now."

"Not true!" Kyle countered, already pulling out his phone. "A really good distraction might help your diagnosis. Plus, I think Katy has a tour stop In Ontario in weeks...not too far from us either."

A wave of nausea washed over Frederick. This was rapidly becoming a situation he couldn't control. He snatched a ragged breath. "What if I...what if I don't feel up to it on the day? Tickets are expensive."

Kyle's eyes held a flicker of concern, the unspoken question echoing in the sudden silence. Was there something more behind Frederick's hesitation, something he wasn't sharing?

Frederick swallowed, a surge of anger bubbling up within him. Anger at the disease, at his own failing body, at Kyle's well-meaning yet clueless intrusion.

He couldn't share the dark thoughts circling his mind - not yet.

"Or...what if I get sick in the crowd? You know how crowded it gets," he sputtered, grasping at straws. The words were half-truths, masking the stark reality of his ever-present fear of debilitating pain or a sudden, humiliating episode in public.

Kyle's brow furrowed further. "We could get seats, find a spot away from the main crowd..." The determination in his friend's eyes sparked a flare of resentment within Frederick. Why couldn't Kyle just understand, and accept without all of this prodding?

"Look, Kyle, I appreciate you thinking of me. But can we just...leave it here, Please?" His voice was tinged with an edge, the frustration leaking through his facade.

The air between them crackled with tension. The shared music now felt like static, a mockery of the once-easy camaraderie. Kyle hesitated, a brief flash of hurt crossing his face before he nodded silently, turning back to the path ahead.

At this point, Frederick knew the tension was going downhill from there. He had to give his friend clarity, something to ease them back to how they had started. In the heat of the moment, he slowed his pace to Kyle's oblivion, the haunting words forming on the tip of his tongue. The running had become a pretense, a way to momentarily outrun the inevitable. But now, their steps slowing to a walk, the truth clawed its way forward.

"Kyle, I need to tell you something," he began, his voice barely a whisper. He couldn't meet his friend's gaze, eyes scanning the familiar park trail, searching for an escape he knew didn't exist. "I've been looking into...assisted dying."

The silence that followed was deafening. Despite his suspicions, part of Kyle hoped he'd been wrong. Now, the dam had broken, and the full reality of Frederick's despair flowed between them.

His breath hitched in his chest, a thousand thoughts battling for dominance. MAiD. It was not an unfamiliar concept – as a doctor, he'd navigated these conversations before. But never like this. Never with his friend.

"Freddie..." was all he could manage, the familiar nickname a weak attempt to bridge the gulf that had suddenly opened between them.

Frederick's gaze finally met his, and the sheer hopelessness in his eyes took Kyle's breath away. "I need you to support me on this Kyle, I need your help, Please." A tremor ran through his voice, his hands twisting together in a futile attempt to control the uncontrollable. "The cancer is winning... I can feel it." He choked, swallowing back the sob that threatened to escape. "I can't let it...I refuse to become a shadow of a person."

Kyle's mind raced, a kaleidoscope of clinical guidelines and agonizing personal loyalty. The oncologist in him wanted to offer options, alternative treatments, and a sliver of hope. But the friend, the one who had shared laughter and late-night calls all through his time in this neighborhood, saw the desperation behind Frederick's eyes. He knew how to recognize when there was no fight left.

"Martha..." The name slipped out before he could censor it. "What about her?"

Frederick winced. "She...she'll understand. Eventually." His voice held a note of uncertainty as if even he didn't quite believe his own words.

Kyle's heart ached. He knew how much Frederick loved his wife, and knew how their love had been a constant through the chaos of the illness. But the clinical side of him couldn't ignore the damage this would leave in its wake.

A surge of defiance rose in Frederick, a spark of his former self. "She will survive, Kyle. We're stronger than we think." But the words rang hollow even in his ears.

Without further conversation, he turned and broke into a sudden sprint, his movements jerky and uncoordinated. It was a desperate escape, a pitiful attempt to outrun the darkness closing in.

As Kyle watched the retreating figure, a wave of anguish washed over him. Their roles had shifted, the patient sprinting ahead, leaving the doctor standing in the dust, burdened with a choice he never wished to make.

Sometimes Waking Up Hurts More

Kyle opened his eyes to a world that shone as harshly as it was familiar. A cacophony of music and disjointed laughter crashed over him, drowning out his disoriented thoughts. The stench of cheap liquor and sweat hung heavy in the air, a sickening mix that made his stomach churn.

He was at a party - that much was clear. But this wasn't a celebration; it was a throbbing, pulsing beast of a thing. Bodies moved in jerky flickers under strobe lights that painted the world in harsh reds and blues. Conversations were lost in drunken slurs, a single word occasionally piercing the din.

Kyle blinked, trying to make sense of it all. He felt dislodged as if abruptly thrust into a play where he knew neither the lines nor the plot. He searched for familiar faces, landmarks, anything that might anchor him. But a sense of wrongness permeated the scene, an undercurrent of unease that sent a shiver down his spine.

A surge of panic pushed him through the crowd. "Martens," he called out, a plea lost in the deafening roar of music. He felt the faint trace of alcohol on his breath. He hadn't been drinking, had he?

A girl with neon-streaked hair bumped into him, giggling in apology. "Looking for someone?" Her words were slurred, eyes dancing with amusement as he described Martens to her. "Maybe I saw them... can't quite remember who..."

He recoiled, frustration building. Each encounter was a dead end – playful dismissals from strangers lost in their revelry, vacant stares from those too sober to recognize the name. The room seemed to spin, a dizzying carousel of strangers.

He needed to find Martens. A sense of urgency, a pull he couldn't explain, propelled him onward. The crowd parted, and finally, a flicker of recognition. There, leaning against the bar on the balcony, was his friend. But the smile usually playing on Martens' lips was replaced by a grim line. It was a Martens he had long tried to forget.

"I can't do this anymore!" Martens' voice, once a source of easy laughter, was a broken rasp. He stared at Kyle with empty eyes, the ghost of their shared dream burning out. "The tests, the pressure...it's crushing me. Remember that anatomy exam? I thought I was going to lose my scholarship..."

Kyle's heart clenched. He remembered Martens' panic before the exam, the sleepless nights, the dark circles that never seemed to fade. They were just kids back then, overwhelmed by the relentless grind.

He reached out, a desperate plea catching in his throat. "Martens, stop this! Don't you see...we need you..." But the crowd surged between them, a faceless mob oblivious to the tragedy unfolding. With each step, he felt himself sinking, a frantic scramble against unseen forces.

"We'll help you," Kyle shouted, his voice barely a whisper above the din. "We'll study, find tutors...there's always a way." But a sickening realization washed over him. Could band-aid solutions ever truly heal his friend's spirit? Did Kyle himself secretly fear this kind of suffocating pressure?

Martens let out a bitter laugh, echoing the cynicism Kyle had once fought so hard to dispel. "It's not just the grades, Kyle. It's everything. The endless nights, the pain...Did we even know what we were signing up for?"

A memory flickered – a late-night shift, the stench of disinfectant, their exhaustion a shared badge of honor. Was that when it began – the slow chipping away at Martens' optimism? Was he now staring at the same terrifying future?

"Martens, listen..." Kyle tried to reach out, a garbled plea forming on his lips. But then he saw it – the balcony. Martens stood precariously close to the edge, moonlight glinting off the metal railing. A scream lodged in Kyle's throat, frozen as he watched his friend teeter on the brink.

The scent hit him then, a wave of cheap cologne mixed with something sharper, a chemical tang. A flash of memory... a late-night shift, the sterile smell of a hospital room...it was the same.

Kyle lunged forward to the plastered remains of his friend, the world lurching violently, and then − darkness. He bolted upright, heart pounding, breath ragged in his ears. The scent lingered for a moment, a phantom in the familiar scent of clean sheets. The dream, always the dream, vanished like mist, leaving nothing but a lingering tremor in his hands and a chilling emptiness in his chest. He desperately tried to blink away the images, but a single tear escaped, tracing a burning path down his cheek.

"Kyle?" Julie's voice cut through the silence, soft and laced with concern. He turned to see her in the dim room light, her brow furrowed. Had his scream ripped her from sleep again?

He forced a shaky breath. "It was nothing. Just a bad dream." The lie caught in his throat, a bitter echo of countless other nights.

Julie sat on the edge of the bed, her warmth a stark contrast to the cold fear that clutched him. She hesitated, a flicker of frustration crossing her features before smoothing them into gentle concern. "It's these nightmares again, isn't it, Kyle?"

The phrasing, the carefully neutral tone, hinted at long conversations they'd danced around but never truly had. Kyle ached to share the burden, to spill the horrors of his recurring dream and the guilt it unearthed. Instead, he averted his gaze, staring out the window where the last remnants of the night were fading into the promise of a new day.

"I'm fine," he said, the word devoid of any true conviction. "Just a rough night, is all."

Julie's sigh was barely audible. "Maybe it's time to see someone about these nightmares."

Her words hung heavy in the air, an unspoken plea for honesty. A part of him wanted to surrender, to let her into the shadowed corners of his mind. But a fierce resistance flared within him. Talking wouldn't bring Martens back. It wouldn't erase the helpless feeling that haunted him every day in the hospital and now seeped into his dreams.

He forced a smile, the brittle facade he knew she could see right through. "I appreciate it, Honey, but... I'll manage." He reached for her hand, clinging to the familiar touch. "Everything will be alright."

The lie hovered between them. Julie didn't push further. Instead, she simply scooted closer, an unspoken offer of comfort he did not fully deserve. They lay there, the silence of their bedroom a vast chasm between their shared bed and the private battle raging within him.

As the first sliver of dawn peeked through the curtains, exhaustion finally claimed him. But even as his eyes drifted shut, the echoes of his desperation still rang in his ears – a broken promise that he couldn't keep even in his dreams.

Crossing the Line

The sterile scent of disinfectant back at the hospital hung heavy in the air, a grim mockery of the warmth and healing it was supposed to represent. Martha, Frederick's wife, came on her own to see Kyle this time. She sat across from him, her usually vibrant presence now muted as her hands nervously fidgeted with her wedding band, its familiar gleam contrasting sharply with the clinical setting.

"Everything's alright at home, I presume?" Kyle asked his voice in an awkward attempt to break the thick silence.

Martha's eyes met his for a brief moment, then flickered away. "I...I think I need help, Kyle," she said, her voice barely above a whisper as he threw her a puzzled look. "You know, sleeping pills, antidepressants, maybe. Or something...stronger."

The request hit him like a gut punch. Depression wasn't unheard of for loved ones of cancer patients, but a self-diagnosis and a prescription from him felt like crossing a line. This wasn't just his friend's wife anymore; she wanted to be his patient, blurring the boundaries even further.

"Martha, I'm not sure that's going..." he began, searching the clinical confines of his mind for the textbook answer that never seemed to exist in real life.

A flicker of frustration flashed across her features. "Wait before you refuse me, I need to say something" She cut him off and positioned herself on his office chair "I don't know if you have heard but Frederick and I haven't been the happiest ever since his diagnosis. Honestly, it's like living with a stranger. Sometimes he's withdrawn, and angry. Then there are moments where it's like he already...gave up on himself, on us."

The words hung between them, unspoken yet deafening. Kyle shifted in his chair, the cool leather doing nothing to ease the sweat prickling on his skin. He needed to tread carefully and offer empathy without overstepping professional boundaries.

"This is incredibly hard on all of you, I know," he said carefully. "But Martha, I'm an oncologist. Depression..."

Her voice, now tinged with a hint of desperation, cut him off. "I know it's not your area, I'm not an idiot. Although I may be depressed I wouldn't come to you for a diagnosis. But you're his doctor. You're the only one he listens to anymore. Please," her eyes held a raw plea that echoed the turmoil in his own heart. "Can't you just...talk to him? For me."

Kyle swallowed, a battle raging within him. He longed to ease Martha's pain, to offer a thread of hope. Yet his professional oath whispered a warning - he couldn't betray Frederick's trust, even if it was for his good.

"It's not that simple," he began, hating the weakness in his voice. But before he could fully explain, the floodgates seemed to open.

Martha's carefully maintained composure crumbled. "It's like he doesn't even care about me anymore, Kyle. He snaps at the kids, barely eats, and just locks himself away. And there are times…times when I fear..." She trailed off, tears streaming silently down her face.

An agonizing mix of guilt and dread washed over Kyle. Martha's pain mirrored his own, and something in the depths of her haunted eyes told him she might have glimpsed the same darkness he saw in Frederick.

Desperate to offer some comfort, he chose his next words with the utmost care. But even so, a hint of the truth seemed to slip through. "This battle can feel so lonely for everybody, Martha," he said, his voice low. "The cancer is taking a toll on him and speaking from experience that is probably the scariest thing that can happen to anybody. So in whatever time he has left, I want you to actively reach out and be there for him. Talk to him more, give him hope. I need you to make him choose to stay with us a little longer."

The request hung heavy between them, a spectre casting a long shadow over the clinical room. "What...what did you mean by that, Kyle?" Martha's voice was barely a whisper now, laced with a mix of fear and a fragile hope she desperately clung to. "Wait, is my husband dying?"

Kyle stared at his clasped hands, a knot tightening in his stomach. He'd crossed a line, a violation of both Frederick's trust and his professional code. The mask of composure he wore with such ease felt brittle, ready to crack into a thousand pieces.

"I, I..." The words seemed caught in his throat, each syllable a confession of his failure. He wanted to apologize and explain that he had spoken out of turn, driven by concern. Yet, another part of him recognized the futility of such excuses.

Martha slowly rose from her chair, her movements stiff, as if the realization had drained her of all strength. "You know something, don't you?" Her voice, once filled with desperation, now held a chilling certainty. "Frederick has been talking to you, hasn't he…"? She could not bring herself to finish the sentence, unspoken words from both parties lingering in the charged silence.

Kyle averted his gaze, shame washing over him in a relentless wave. The truth burned behind his tightly closed eyes, a haunting image of Frederick's despairing face as he revealed his intentions to him.

A tremor ran through Martha's body as the full weight of the situation crashed down upon her. The tears came then, not the silent streams from before, but ragged sobs that echoed with primal grief. She fumbled for her purse, movements jerky and uncoordinated.

"I…I have to go," she choked out, her voice thick with unshed tears. The accusation in her eyes was sharper than any rebuke she could have spoken aloud.

She turned and fled the room, her retreating footsteps a painful picture marking Kyle's failure.

The door clicked shut behind her, leaving him enveloped in silence, a silence that shrieked louder than any words.

His carefully crafted world had tilted on its axis. He'd broken Frederick's trust and violated the sacred oath he'd sworn to uphold. He'd risked it all, driven by a misguided attempt to help, and now he was left with the wreckage - shattered trust and a lingering dread for the consequences his slip of the tongue could have for Frederick, for Martha, for himself.

A single thought echoed in his chaotic mind: What have I done? The answer, bleak and terrifying, remained elusive, lost in a future that suddenly seemed fraught with despair.

The Collapse

The rhythmic rattle of the dryer seemed to mock the growing discord in the room. Frederick, hunched over a crossword puzzle, appeared oblivious to the storm brewing within Martha. For him, this was just another day in their new life. With a sigh that rippled through the tense silence, Martha yanked open the dryer door, a cloud of steam billowing out like a frustrated exhale.

"Seriously, Frederick?" she said, holding up a crumpled, misshapen shirt. "How many times do I have to tell you to separate the delicates?"

Frederick glanced up, his brow furrowed in irritation. "I thought I did," he mumbled, barely looking away from the puzzle.

"Thought you did?" Martha echoed, her voice laced with a sharp edge. "That's the problem, isn't it? Assumptions. Never actually doing the work, just assuming someone else will clean up the mess."

Frederick's pen snapped as his frustration mirrored hers. "Come on, Martha. Don't make a mountain out of a molehill, they're just clothes."

"You know it's always just that simple to you?" Her voice was low, a tremor of anger shaking her hand. "But have you ever stopped to think about me?"

He finally looked up, his gaze meeting hers. The defiance in his eyes instantly crumbled, replaced by a flicker of fear. "What are you talking about?"

Martha took a deep breath, the words churning in her stomach. This wasn't how she'd planned it, but the dam had finally broken. "I went to see Kyle today," she blurted out, the pronouncement hanging heavy in the air.

Frederick's face drained of color. The crossword puzzle slipped from his grasp, scattering papers across the floor. He stared at her, his eyes wide with a mix of terror and betrayal.

"What did you just say?" His voice was barely a whisper, laced with fear and a hint of desperation.

Martha drew herself up, her resolve hardening with each passing second. "You heard me, Frederick," she said, her voice stronger now. "Don't make me repeat myself. What did you talk to Kyle about?"

A flicker of panic darted across Frederick's face. "I don't understand what you mean," he retorted, his words lacking any conviction.

"Don't insult me, Frederick!" Martha's words were a whiplash. "He slipped. His professional mask cracked, just for a moment, and I saw the truth in his eyes." She took a step towards him, the laundry basket forgotten on the floor. "What are you planning?"

Guilt washed over Frederick, his shoulders slumping in defeat. With a choked sob, he admitted, "I've been thinking...about options. More permanent options for this... my disease." He noticed the look in her eyes, judging him "Come on Martha, It's my body, my decision."

"Your decision?" Martha scoffed, her voice dripping with bitter disbelief. And what about us? What about your children?"

"They know I'm suffering enough already. Trust me they'll understand. Eventually." The words hung hollow in the air, lacking the bravado he sought. "This cancer…it's taking everything from me. I'm not…I'm not a man anymore."

Martha flinched as if slapped. "So you'd give up so easily? Just discard the love, the family, a life we fought so hard to build…"

"It's not giving up!" Frederick retorted, his voice rising. "It's taking control. Choosing when this nightmare ends before it destroys every shred of who I am!"

The accusation hung between them, shattering the illusion of normalcy. Frederick's attempts at defence dwindled in the face of Martha's anguished stare.

"How could you?" Martha's voice cracked, the anger in her eyes giving way to a profound despair. "After everything – the fight, the hope we held onto…you'd just throw it away?" Tears welled up, threatening to spill over as the magnitude of his decision sank deep within her.

Frederick flinched, each of her words a blow to his already battered spirit. "It's not that simple," he began a desperate attempt to explain the unexplainable. "You don't see it, Martha…the emptiness."

"Emptiness?" Martha's voice was thick with scorn and sorrow. "You dare speak of emptiness? When what you're doing would leave a void in our lives so vast, it would swallow us whole?" She closed the distance between them, her voice now a plea. "Frederick, please…fight. Fight with me, like we always have."

A spasm of pain wracked Frederick's body. A sharp cough tore from his throat, followed by a series of choked gasps. He leaned heavily against the countertop, a sheen of sweat breaking out on his brow.

Martha's heart clenched in fear. This was more than exhaustion, more than the relentless toll of the cancer. Their heated exchange had tipped the fragile balance, pushing Frederick's ravaged body to its limits.

"Frederick?" Her voice was barely a whisper, laced with sudden dread. His trembling hand clutched at his chest, his breaths growing increasingly shallow. A wave of nausea washed over her, the realization of what she'd done threatening to shatter her resolve. The argument seemed insignificant now, a petty squabble in the face of his faltering health.

The void they were teetering on the edge of seemed bottomless, consuming. Frederick's body went rigid, his eyes rolling back in his head. A strangled cry escaped his lips before he collapsed, a sickening thud echoing against the tiled floor.

Martha stood frozen, a scream caught in her throat. A terrifying numbness washed over her as the stark reality replaced her fragmented thoughts.

She stumbled forward, her hands trembling as she knelt beside him.

"Frederick, no…please!" Tears streamed down her face, hot and relentless. His body convulsed violently, an unnatural rhythm that shook her to the core. His skin took on a ghastly pallor, his lips turning a chilling shade of blue.

A jolt of adrenaline surged through her. Fear morphed into a primal instinct, the fight for survival eclipsing the overwhelming despair. With a trembling hand, she fumbled for her phone, its sterile white light a stark contrast to the unfolding horror.

"9-1-1!" The words were a ragged plea. "My husband…he's having a seizure…please hurry!" Her voice, usually resolute and strong, faltered under the strain.

Panic clawed at her, constricting her breathing, each passing second an eternity. Should she wait? No, every moment was precious. With newfound determination, she scooped Frederick into her arms, his weight a terrible burden in their familiar embrace.

She staggered towards the car, a whirlwind of terror propelling her forward. The keys slipped through her trembling fingers, the clatter reverberating in the empty garage. Her vision blurred, and threats and regrets were a dissonant chorus in her mind.

The engine roared to life, her foot slammed against the accelerator. The world outside was a hazy blur, her focus solely on the hospital, a beacon of hope in the rapidly descending darkness.

The Call That Seals a Fate

The antiseptic smell of the hospital room clung to Kyle like a suffocating shroud. Monitors beeped rhythmically, each electronic pulse a reminder of his friend's precarious hold on life. Frederick lay propped against crisp white sheets, shockingly frail, the vibrant man Kyle once knew reduced to a pale shadow. Yet, Frederick's eyes held a chilling determination that cut through any illusion of vulnerability.

"Thank you for coming, Kyle." Frederick's voice was a harsh rasp, each laboured breath a testament to his weak body.

Kyle nodded, the words of reassurance he wanted to offer choking in his throat. He reached out cautiously, taking Frederick's calloused hand in his, the warmth a stark contrast to his clinical surroundings.

"The seizure...it changes nothing," Frederick continued, his gaze unwavering. "This…this thing inside me...it's a cruel master." A flicker of pain crossed his features, a spasm wracking his weakened frame.

A wave of nausea washed over Kyle. A flashback – the same pallor, the hopeless pleading in those dimming eyes – he was watching Martens die again. And now, the cruel echo of that final helpless battle played out before him.

"Frederick, it doesn't have to be this way," Kyle began, his voice laced with a desperate hope he didn't truly feel. "We haven't exhausted all the options. There's still…"

Frederick squeezed his hand, a fleeting show of gratitude. "Kyle, please. Didn't you hear what Martha had said? Don't make this harder than it already is." His voice, though faint, held a chilling finality.

"But I am not coming to you as a patient but as a friend." Frederick managed a retort. "Think of it as my dying wish, the last thing I need to do."

Silence hung between them, heavy and oppressive. The monitors seemed to blare in accusation, each beat a countdown neither could ignore. This wasn't a doctor-patient conversation anymore. This was a plea between friends, a battle between life and the cold, stark reality of death's looming presence.

***

The phone lay on the bedside table, an innocuous black rectangle transformed into a harbinger of irreversible decisions. Kyle's hand hovered above it, trembling with a mixture of dread and resignation he battled to accept. The echo of Martha's anguished plea rang in his ears.

Hadn't he fought, tooth and nail, for both Frederick and Martens? Failure gnawed at him, amplified by the memory of a wasted, crumpled body on a different hospital bed, in a different room years ago. He had lost that battle, and the bitter taste of defeat lingered.

With a shuddering breath, he picked up the phone. His fingers, clumsy and cold, fumbled with the familiar keypad, each tap a countdown to a predetermined destiny he was powerless to stop.

"Hello, Hilda?" His voice was barely a whisper, thin and strained.

"Kyle? It's been quite some time." Hilda's voice was smooth, her tone measured. Compassion seeped through, yet a hint of clinical detachment lingered, a necessary armor for the work she did.

"Yes, it has," Kyle replied, a heavy weight settling in his stomach. "I... I have a patient. He's...he's been struggling for a long time, and... he can't bring himself, to fight anymore, so his final request is for assisted dying."

Perhaps Hilda sensed his turmoil in explaining this because she replied. "It's alright, Kyle. I understand. It's what I do for a living." There was a gentleness in her tone now, offering a tentative comfort. "Would an appointment at the hospital tomorrow be okay?"

"Yes," He steeled himself, and a sliver of hope reignited. "Hilda, I just want you to know that I haven't forgotten what happened with your brother, Martens... so if you might not be up to it I'll totally..."

"Kyle, please." Her voice sharpened, the understanding dissolving. "That was in the past, different time, different suicide. Besides, this must be your patient's choice, freely made."

"Yes... Yes, it is," Kyle's last resignation died on his lips. He knew she was right, yet the responsibility still felt like a noose tightening around his neck.

"So see you tomorrow...Bye..." The call ended, the silence ringing louder than any dial tone. Kyle hung up the phone, her words echoing ominously in the sterile room. All he had to do was get some very much-needed sleep, but something in him knew that the profound choice he had just facilitated wouldn't let him.

A Ghost That Never Left

Dr. Hilda Tennant entered Kyle's office, a somber echo of her twin brother. The same dark hair, and the same steady gaze, yet something behind her eyes was profoundly different. While Martens radiated youthful energy, Hilda carried a quiet maturity that seemed to press down on her with the wait of ten years.

The moment she'd arrived, Kyle rose to greet her, the ghost of their shared relation standing unspoken between them. His stomach churned a cocktail of guilt and a desperate hope that she wouldn't discern the truth of all those years ago.

"Dr. Tennant," He spoke the same name he had used to mock Martens all those years ago. "Thank you for coming on such short notice," he said, his voice slightly strained.

She nodded a touch of warmth in her expression easing a fraction of his anxiety. "Of course, Doctor. I understand the urgency."

They settled into the stiff office chairs, clinical charts, and paperwork a stark barrier between them. Kyle cleared his throat, forcing himself back into the familiar role of the oncologist.

"As you know, Mr. Carter..." he hesitated, unsure of how much Hilda knew about Frederick's decision. "Your patient is a middle-aged male diagnosed with advanced pancreatic cancer..." He recited the clinical details he knew by heart, the words feeling strangely hollow against the weight of the situation.

Kyle's eyes flickered towards Hilda, gauging her reaction. Her professional mask held firm, though he thought he detected a flicker of sadness as he described Frederick's deteriorating condition, the relentless decline that mirrored her brother's final weeks.

He reached for Frederick's chart, his hands trembling slightly. "Would you like to see him? Discuss the procedure, explain…" He couldn't bring himself to say the words "assisted dying" in her presence.

Hilda rose, her movements composed. "Yes, I believe that would be best." A flicker of understanding passed between them, a silent acknowledgment of the gravity of their task.

Together, they walked down the hospital corridor towards Frederick's room. Kyle felt a growing sense of dread, each step bringing him closer to the moment he would have to witness his friend's final choice.

As they entered the room, Frederick looked up, a flicker of recognition in his eyes. Hilda approached his bedside, her voice soft and soothing. "Mr. Carter, my name is Dr. Tennant. I've been asked to help you…"

Her words trailed off, replaced by a quiet conversation Kyle felt unable to intrude upon. He watched as Hilda explained the procedure, her gentle manner offering a sliver of comfort in the face of the inevitable. Frederick, though visibly weakened, seemed to find a strange solace in Hilda's presence. His gaze drifted towards the window, as if contemplating a future he would never have.

Exiting Frederick's room, they walked in step, the weight of the situation hanging heavy between them. The usually bustling hospital corridor seemed muffled, the distant echoes of monitors and announcements a stark contrast to the profound silence that enveloped them.

"Umm, have you seen that reunion ad... you know for our med school class of '14" Kyle was struggling to find the words but seemed to manage it. But to his surprise, Hilda answered nonchalantly.

"Yeah, it sounds like it's going to be fun..."

"Well, I wouldn't know because I'm not going." He blurted, eager to release the words from his mouth.

"Even though it's also Marten's memorial?" Hilda said, throwing him a suspicious look. "Well I think you should go, but it's not on me to make that choice for you." Her voice was gentle but firm. It wasn't a suggestion but a statement filled with a deep understanding of hidden wounds.

Kyle felt a surge of guilt wash over him. "The thing is, I don't know if I can. That day...it…" He choked back the words, the image of Martens' lifeless body seared into his memory. "It changed something in me. I don't know if I'm strong enough to face it all again."

They reached Kyle's office. He gestured for her to sit, a wave of exhaustion washing over him as he took his seat. The familiar surroundings offered no solace, the framed medical certificates on the wall a mocking testament to his oath to do whatever it took to save lives.

"You know Martens' death…it wasn't your fault right?" Hilda said quietly, shattering the illusion of composure he clung to.

The words stung, a self-inflicted wound he'd kept hidden for so long. If only she knew the truth... She wouldn't be talking like this.

"But I should have seen the signs. The depression, the withdrawal...I failed him, first as his friend and then as a doctor."

Tears pricked at the corners of his eyes, a testament to the relentless burden he carried. "An aspiring doctor." She corrected " We were all still in training back then."

"Yes, but I chose this profession to heal, to fight for people. But now..." he gestured helplessly, unable to complete the thought.

"You know what I've learned, Kyle? Sometimes we win, but most times we lose and that's okay," Hilda interjected, her voice laced with her understanding of that bitter reality.

A sob escaped Kyle's throat. "So? Do I just go on, picking up the pieces, knowing I couldn't stop the inevitable?"

Hilda leaned forward, her gaze unwavering. "You just said it yourself, 'the inevitable'. How can you stop something that is already meant to be? As doctors, we carry the burden of 'the inevitable'. That's the nature of our work. But we can't let it crush us."

She reached into her bag, retrieving a small card. "After Martens…I couldn't go on either. The grief was too heavy. That's when I found Dr. Simmons." She handed him the card, the name of a therapist, and a phone number scrawled on it.

"She's not just a therapist," Hilda continued. "She specializes in trauma and…and burnout."

Kyle stared at the card, the weight of it mirroring his burden. "I…I don't know…"

"You owe it to yourself, Kyle. To Martens. And to all the patients you'll help in the future." Hilda paused, a touch of warmth entering her voice. "Besides, I'd like to see you at my brother's memorial. I think we could both use a friend right now."

The Burden of Memory

The therapist's office was a world away from the sterile hospital environment that had become Kyle's second home. Here, soft lighting bathed the room in a gentle glow, and plush chairs promised comfort, not clinical assessment. A faint scent of lavender hung in the air, a subtle balm for frayed nerves.

Kyle sank into the armchair, his body protesting the unfamiliar softness. The worn leather of his satchel felt reassuring in his grip, a tether to the world of medical charts and certainties he understood. The framed diplomas and certificates on the therapist's wall seemed out of place, irrelevant to the internal battle waging within him Dr. Simmons smiled warmly. "I'm glad you decided to come, Kyle." Her voice was smooth and calming, effortlessly easing a fraction of his anxiety. "Is this your first experience with…this type of therapy?"

He hesitated, the weight of the question making his shoulders slump. "I've…spoken to people before. After Martens." There was a hollowness to the words, a reminder of failed attempts to find solace.

"And did it help?" Dr. Simmons tilted her head slightly, her gaze compassionate but probing.

Kyle averted his eyes. "Not really. It all felt…forced. Like reciting a well-rehearsed script."

"That's understandable." Dr. Simmons nodded, her expression thoughtful. "Hmm, trauma has a way of defying words. Hypnosis allows us to go beyond words, accessing memories your conscious mind might suppress for protection."

The idea was both intriguing and terrifying. "Suppress?" Kyle echoed. "You mean, I might be hiding things from myself?"

Dr. Simmons chose her words carefully. "Perhaps a different way of seeing things. A chance to reconnect with the full emotional truth of an experience." She paused, letting the implications sink in. "Of course, only if you're ready."

He stared at his clenched hands, the memory of Martens' lifeline slipping through his fingers vivid in his mind. "I don't know if I'll ever be ready," he confessed in a strained voice. "But I can't keep going on like this. Drowning in something I don't even fully understand."

Dr. Simmons offered him a reassuring smile. "That's why we're here, Kyle. To dive into those murky depths together. Are you willing to take that first step?"

Dr. Simmons' voice guided him gently, her words a lullaby leading him back to a night etched in his memory. "Close your eyes, Kyle. Breathe slowly and deeply. Feel your body relaxing, sinking deeper…deeper into this moment of stillness."

The room dissolved, the scent of lavender replaced by the stale reek of cheap alcohol and the pulsating thrum of music that pounded against his skull. He was back at the party, the same overwhelming chaos enveloping him like one of his dreams. The disjointed laughter, the strobe lights flashing like jagged lightning, the blurred faces of strangers – it all came rushing back with a terrifying intensity.

"Find Martens," Dr. Simmons instructed her voice distant yet grounding. "Where is he?"

Kyle felt himself moving through the crowd, a frantic surge of panic mirroring his past desperation. "Martens," he called out, a strangled whisper lost amidst the cacophony. He reached the balcony, and there he was, a silhouette outlined against the city lights, perched precariously on the weathered railing.

"It's over, Kyle," Martens slurred, his voice a chilling echo of despair. "The fight, the pretending, all of it...none of it matters anymore."

A surge of adrenaline propelled Kyle forward. "Martens, stop! Don't do this!" he pleaded, the words catching in his throat.

But it was too late. With a sickening lurch that mirrored Kyle's own heart, Martens flung himself into the void.

Kyle gasped, his body jolting in the armchair. "No!" he shouted, reaching out with desperate, trembling hands.

"Kyle, breathe," Dr. Simmons urged, her voice firm but soothing. "You're safe. It's just a memory. Breathe."

But the memory was transforming, shifting into something horrifyingly new. As Martens fell, Kyle, in a primal act of desperation, caught his forearm, the slippery fabric of Martens' jacket the only barrier between life and oblivion.

"Kyle, please! Help me!" Martens' voice, hoarse with terror, cut through the relentless music.

Kyle's muscles burned with the strain, his own body precariously balanced. His fingers began to slip, sweat making the hold treacherous. Time morphed into a suffocating eternity, each second weighing him down with agonizing inevitability.

A choked sob escaped his lips. "I can't hold on! I'm so sorry..." He felt Martens' grip loosen, the weight suddenly shifting. An anguished scream tore from his throat as he watched his friend plunge into the darkness below.

The room swayed, the gentle scent of lavender replaced by the metallic tang of blood. His hands were slick with a phantom chill, the ghostly echo of his failure a chilling stain on his soul.

Kyle collapsed back into the present, his body wracked with uncontrollable sobs. Tears streamed down his face, hot and relentless. The weight of the revelation was crushing, a burden far heavier than the imagined guilt he'd carried all these years.

Through the haze of his emotional storm, he felt Dr. Simmons' presence, a gentle hand on his shoulder. "It's alright, Kyle. Let it out," she murmured, her voice a beacon in the darkness that threatened to engulf him.

The aftermath of the hypnosis was a raw, exposed wound. Each shuddering breath ached in his lungs, his body a physical testament to the emotional turmoil he'd unleashed. Dr. Simmons waited patiently, offering tissues and silent support.

"I tried to save him," Kyle finally rasped, his voice a broken scratch. "I tried…"

"Yes, you did, Kyle," Dr. Simmons said gently. "And sometimes, even with our best efforts, the worst happens. This wasn't your fault."

The words were like a balm, but a burning one. He thought of the simplified version he'd repeated over the years, the comfortable lie easing the burden of blame. The truth was far more complex, an agonizing mix of guilt, self-preservation, and the futile desire to protect the memory of his friend.

"Kyle," Dr. Simmons nudged him gently, "it's understandable to feel shame, even anger. You were in an impossible situation." She gave him a knowing look. "Perhaps part of you believed…if you kept the truth hidden, even from yourself, it would somehow lessen your responsibility."

A bitter laugh escaped his lips. "Does it? Does knowing the whole truth make it hurt any less?"

"Perhaps not less," Dr. Simmons conceded, "but differently. You were never to blame for Martens' choice. But now, you're no longer carrying the weight of a hidden falsehood. That's a crucial step towards healing."

The vibration of his phone brought a jarring intrusion. He fumbled with numb fingers, a PET scan result flashing across the screen. Patient: Frederick Carter. The name was a thunderclap, a stark reminder of his impending failure, the promises about to be broken.

A surge of adrenaline shot through him, cutting through the emotional fog. "It's the PET scan results of one of my patients. Oh my God! I have to go!" he said, a sense of desperate hope replacing the despair.

Dr. Simmons looked at him with a curious smile. "Whoa! Where are you in such a rush to?"

The words seemed to hang in the air, a question he was addressing to himself as much as to her. "To save a life," he said, determination in his voice, "for real this time."

The Bane is Lifted

A hush had fallen over the hospital ward, a sterile silence punctuated by the rhythmic beeps of monitors. Frederick lay motionless, a figure lost against the crisp white sheets. The air was heavy with the unspoken knowledge of the impending procedure, a finality both terrible and unavoidable.

Then all of a sudden single, tentative note pierced the silence. A melody began to form, a soft, mournful tune that seemed oddly familiar to Frederick, yet still somewhat distant. A flicker of confusion crossed Frederick's face, an echo of recognition before comprehension.

"...another life, I would be your girl," a voice drifted into the room, laced with a quiet ache. The melody grew stronger, the words more distinct, carrying a bittersweet edge that tugged at buried memories.

"We'd keep all our promises, be us against the world." Hilda glanced towards Frederick, a question in her eyes. "Do you..."

"I don't know," he whispered, his gaze searching the space beyond the doorway. The song swirled around him, each note a painful echo of a past he'd almost forsaken.

Then he saw her, Martha standing in the doorway, her frame trembling slightly. Her eyes locked with Frederick's, and the lyrics poured from her lips, a raw plea for another chance. "In another life, I would make you stay, so I don't have to say, you were the one that got away..."

Tears welled up in Frederick's eyes as the song's full meaning hit him. And from the depths of his despair, his voice joined hers, first in a soft murmur, then rising stronger with a tremor that echoed her own. "The one that got away..."

The melody lingered in the air, a moment of connection amidst the bleak reality. Then ever so suddenly, Kyle burst into the room, his presence shattering the fragile spell of the music. He froze, caught off guard by the unanticipated scene before him.

Martha gasped, her voice catching mid-note. Frederick stared with a mix of confusion and ecstasy in his eyes. Hilda stood motionless, absorbing the shift in the atmosphere.

"Was I…interrupting something?" Kyle began, his voice laced with a hesitant apology. His gaze fell upon the paper in his hand, the PET scan results suddenly feeling foreign and out of place.

A tense silence stretched, broken only by Frederick's raspy question. "Kyle…what is that?"

"Your PET scan results," Kyle replied, his voice gaining strength. "There's been…a development." He looked at Martha, meeting her hopeful yet questioning gaze, then back at Frederick. "Your cancer…it's in remission."

The words hung in the air, a startling contrast to the minutes before. A gasp escaped Martha's lips.

Frederick blinked, the disbelief clear on his face. "Remission?" he repeated, his voice barely a whisper.

"It's…it seems like a miracle," Kyle fumbled for the right words, his own emotions rising to the surface. "The tumor…it's shrunk significantly. With additional treatment, surgery maybe…there's a real chance." Kyle could barely contain his elation. "A real chance…"

The weight of the newfound hope, sudden and unexpected, pressed down upon Frederick. A battle raged within him, a flicker of newfound determination wrestling with the lingering exhaustion of despair.

"So…does this mean…" Martha's voice trembled hope and fear battling for dominance in her eyes. "Does this mean you're not dying anymore?"

Frederick looked at Hilda, seeking reassurance, seeking permission he no longer knew he needed. Her gaze met his, her expression warm yet purposeful.

"The choice," she said softly, "is still yours to make, Frederick."

He turned to Martha, a flicker of a smile gracing his lips. "I guess," he said, a playful rasp to his voice that seemed a lifetime ago, "I'm not getting away anytime soon."

The words hung heavy with meaning, both a reference to the song's refrain and a testament to the precious gift of more time. A surge of jubilation washed over them - tears of relief, stifled laughter, and profound gratitude for the life yet to be fought for, yet to be lived.

Kyle could feel the happiness swirling around him into his bones, a stark contrast to the turmoil he carried within. Glancing at Hilda, he felt a renewed weight on his shoulders. He couldn't celebrate fully, knowing the truth he still concealed.

As the initial elation subsided, he gently pulled Hilda aside. "Dr. Tennant," he began, his voice strained, "there's something I need to tell you…about Martens."

Hilda's gaze softened a hint of understanding in her eyes. "Let's step outside," she said, leading him into the quiet hospital hallway.

He took a deep breath, the words heavy on his tongue. "That night…with Martens…it wasn't as simple as…as I let people believe." His voice faltered, images of the chaotic scene flashing in his mind.

"He didn't just…fall. I arrived there on time and tried to pull him back," Kyle confessed, the shame and guilt fresh after all these years. "But when I couldn't hold on to him any longer, I… He…" the words kept choking at his throat. "I swear I tried, but I couldn't hold on."

A flicker of surprise, then a wave of understanding washed over Hilda's features. She placed a gentle hand on his arm. "Kyle, you tried to save him. You did all you could."

Tears pricked at Kyle's eyes, a relief unlike any he'd ever felt. "But it wasn't enough."

"Sometimes, it isn't," Hilda said quietly. "But blame does not lessen the pain, for you or anyone else." She looked at him with a warmth that pierced his self-imposed isolation. "You weren't responsible for his choice, Kyle. Just as Frederick isn't responsible for his illness. We can only fight so hard before accepting the limits of our control."

Her words were a balm to his wounded soul. A burden he'd carried for so long began to lighten, replaced with a sliver of newfound acceptance, and perhaps, a path towards self-forgiveness.

The hospital hallway remained tinged with the echoes of celebration as Kyle stood alone this time, basking in the unexpected flicker of a clear conscience that had infused the once somber space. His phone vibrated, breaking through his thoughts. Dr. Simmons' name flashed on the screen.

"Hello?" he answered, a surprising softness replacing the clinical detachment in his voice.

"Kyle, I hope I'm not interrupting," Dr. Simmons said, her voice laced with warmth and a hint of concern. "It's just that you had left in quite a hurry during our last session."

"There was an emergency at the hospital," he replied, a flicker of a smile gracing his lips.

"I can only imagine," Dr. Simmons said, "I just wanted to check if we would have an appointment next week. You know for further examination, " There was a brief silence between them, dancing in the noise of the razzmatazz in Frederick's room.

"Why, Doctor," he affirmed, a newfound determination resonating in his voice. " Of course, I'll be seeing you again next week. My healing…is far from over."

Epilogue

A symphony of laughter and reminiscence filled the conference room, a rowdy energy Kyle's introverted brain couldn't yet comprehend. The reunion had arrived, and while his classmates slipped seamlessly into their old elements, Kyle felt an uncomfortable mix of anticipation and dread. His nerves were partially brought on by the speech he was about to give.

As he stepped aside, the crowd parted, revealing a podium at the front. His nametag was there, calling him to a destiny he both longed for and feared. With a deep breath, he ascended, the buzz of the crowd fading with every step he made away from them. He looked out at the sea of faces – some familiar, others weathered by time and the weight of diverse battles with their shared profession.

"For years," he began, his voice surprisingly steady after weeks of anguished therapy and preparation, "I carried the guilt of everyone I couldn't save. Doctors in the house, you all know what I'm talking about." An awkward laugh erupted from the audience. "Every single friend, family, and sometimes even patients... Their faces haunted my dreams, a relentless reminder of my failure." A collective sigh rippled through the room at the sound of his words, the exhale of those who knew despair in its many forms.

He continued, his words taking on a rhythm of their own. He told them of his grief, not as a textbook definition but as a creature that wrapped its icy tendrils around his heart for a decade. He spoke of burnout, licking at the corners of even the most dedicated souls. And then, he confessed his journey into the depths of therapy.

"We, as doctors, are not immune to pain. We bleed alongside our patients, even while we try desperately to heal their wounds," he declared, the words taking flight, finding purchase in the solemn eyes staring back. Heads nodded in understanding, some eyes damp with tears silently shed for losses far too familiar.

As his speech drew to a close, he felt a warmth flood his veins. It wasn't just the relief of finally sharing his truth; it was a newfound resolve – a knowledge that his journey could ignite a spark of healing within others.

His eyes searched the crowd, staring at the lives he seemed to have touched. Then he found something else, or someone ever so peculiar. A figure in the back row, leaning against the wall. The face... was one he'd recognize anywhere. Martens – youthful, a playful smirk on his lips, a glint of what could have been in his eyes.

Kyle faltered for the merest second, his heart thundering in his chest. Was this a trick of the mind, a cruel echo of unresolved grief? Yet the figure remained, solid and undeniable. With a deliberate nod, Martens turned, his eyes holding Kyle's until he crossed the threshold. He glanced back, a wink creasing the corner of his eye before he disappeared.

Time stuttered, the room tilting like a ship caught in a sudden squall. A sense of calm washed over Kyle, not the feverish heat of guilt, but the slow, steady burn of acceptance. It didn't erase the scars, or promise that darkness wouldn't call again, but the weight felt transformed. The ghost that had haunted him for so long was no longer a shackle but a part of who he had become.

As the applause swelled, he stepped off the stage, feeling steadier than he had in years. He wasn't just a doctor, or a man haunted, or even a cautionary tale come to life. He was walking proof that sometimes, healing comes in moments of vulnerability, and perhaps, in those impossible moments when the veil between what is and what could have been, grows gossamer thin.

About the Author

Storytelling is to Ife Akanegbu what art is to Picasso: an undeniable passion that only grows stronger with each tale told. Born in Nigeria, what began as a means of passing the time for a young boy would soon evolve into a creative outlet when, years later, Ife decided to add his voice to the mental health debate by combining his gift with his vast medical expertise. By covering various topics from health problems and communicable diseases to writing Christian short stories, he is determined to impact lives by inspiring people to start deep and honest discussions on matters that are often considered too difficult to initiate, even as he promotes preventive medicine. Ife is versatile and as dedicated to addressing children through his captivating stories as he is to addressing adults.

Leading a life full of adventure, compassion, and resilience with lots of life lessons along the way, Ife enjoys sharing his thrilling experiences with others. He completed his medical training in Nigeria and obtained his Master's in Health Management at the University of Leeds. Ife now practices family medicine in British Columbia. With more projects in the works, you can certainly look forward to more beautiful, vivid, and interactive reads.

Ife loves connecting with his readers, so feel free to leave a review or comment.

www.mycutestories.com

Manufactured by Amazon.ca
Bolton, ON

39231643R00055